Mein Berlin

Mein Berlin

fotografiert und kommentiert
von
Bernd Ehrig

VERLAG BERND EHRIG

Umschlagbild: Siegessäule
Frontispiz: Kaiser-Wilhelm-Gedächtniskirche
Vorderes Vorsatz: Schloßhof Charlottenburg
Hinteres Vorsatz: Am Wannsee

Cover: Victory Column
Frontispiece: Kaiser-Wilhelm Memorial Church
Front picture inside cover: The courtyard of the Charlottenburg Palace
Back inside cover: At the Wannsee

ENGLISCHE ÜBERSETZUNG:
JOAN MURPHY
SATZ:
ADOLPH FÜRST & SOHN · BERLIN
DRUCK:
BEROSET · BEROLINA OFFSETDRUCK · BERLIN
BINDEARBEITEN:
BUCHBINDEREI GODRY · BERLIN

© 1980 Verlag Bernd Ehrig, Barstraße 28, 1000 Berlin 31
Alle Rechte, einschließlich derjenigen der fotomechanischen Vervielfältigung und des auszugsweisen Nachdrucks, vorbehalten
Printed in Germany
ISBN 3-88407-005-3

Mein Berlin

Der Stoßseufzer kommt von Herzen: 1964 war das nun schon, als ich nach Berlin übersiedelte. Ich gehe die verflossenen Jahre in Gedanken durch, bleibe da und dort hängen, werde ein wenig sentimental und ziehe Bilanz – wie immer, mit dem gleichen Resultat. Recht hatte ich, sage ich mir, daß ich damals gekommen bin und all die zaudernden Spießer hinter mir gelassen habe. Recht hatte ich, wiederhole ich zur Bekräftigung und räume dennoch ein, daß ich ohne allzu große Begeisterung gekommen bin. Meine Gründe waren sozusagen geschäftlich. Leicht könnte ich erhabenere Motive ins Spiel bringen. Ich könnte daran erinnern, daß Berlin drei Jahre nach dem Bau der unglückseligen Mauer Fachkräfte dringend benötigte, ich könnte den Frontstadtcharakter und das besondere politische Bewußtsein ins Feld führen, ja ich könnte ein weiteres Mal die hunderttausendfach bekannten Klischees entwickeln. Doch die Jahre in Berlin haben mich geprägt, über derlei spricht man hier nicht, der Beigeschmack von Pathos wäre gar zu aufdringlich.

Die anfängliche Skepsis meinem neuen Domizil gegenüber wich allmählich. Aus der zunächst sehr nüchternen und sachlichen Beziehung zu Berlin wurde im Verlaufe der folgenden Monate so etwas wie Zuneigung und dann, als der Funke übersprang, sogar Leidenschaft. Inzwischen ist mir längst klar, daß man Berlin nicht im Sturm erobern kann. Dies Ding braucht Weile und niemand weiß das besser, als die vielen Zugereisten, die später Lokalpatrioten aus Überzeugung wurden.

Die vermeintlich glänzende Fassade von Berlin, mit der das hiesige Verkehrsamt lockt, sie ist tatsächlich vorhanden. Nur ist sie eben genauso oberflächlich wie anderswo und gerade für Berlin nicht kennzeichnend. Berlin ist keine üppige Schönheit. Berlin ist auch keine Stadt wie Rom, Paris oder Prag, die Historie und Monumentales in verschwenderischer Fülle darbieten könnte. Berlin gleicht eher einer Frau, nach der man sich nicht umdreht, die aber nichtsdestoweniger Tugenden wie Warmherzigkeit, Mütterlichkeit und Zuverlässigkeit zu bieten hätte.

Mein Verhältnis zu Berlin war deshalb von Anfang an ein wenig zwiespältig. Die sogenannten Sehenswürdigkeiten haben mich nie so recht beeindruckt, das als weltstädtisch Gepriesene hat mich nie geblendet, die Bewohner aber, die Berliner also, die haben mich überzeugt, die sind es, die Berlin zu dieser prächtigen Stadt erhoben haben. Die Berliner sind – man gestatte mir auch dieses Kompliment – aufgeschlossen und tolerant wie kein zweiter Menschenschlag. Man wird mit einem keinesfalls mißtrauischen, eher neugierigen „Wat will der denn hier?" sofort akzeptiert und aufgenommen. Freilich, unaufrichtige Höflichkeitsformeln und falsche Rücksichtnahmen gibt es nicht. So sagte mir die resolute Mittfünfzigerin am Winterfeldtplatz ohne Umschweife ins Gesicht: „Fotografieren wollen Se det hier? Wenn Se hier wohnen müßten, dann fänden Se det bestimmt nich scheen!" Berlinische Ehrlichkeit ist entwaffnend, sie verschlägt umständlichen Provinzlern nicht selten die Sprache, sie ist aber eigentlich nie verletzend gemeint. Ich schätze diese Direktheit, denn sie allein schafft klare Verhältnisse.

Berlin ist eine vergleichsweise junge und unerhört rasch gewachsene Stadt. Wie einst Amerika auf alle unruhigen Geister magische Anziehungskraft ausübte, so war auch Berlin ein menschlicher Schmelztiegel. Amerika trug das den Ruf ein, das Land der unbegrenzten Möglichkeiten zu sein; wer in deutschen Landen was werden wollte, mußte nach Berlin kommen. Neuerer, Intellektuelle, zupackende Handwerker, Künstler und all die, die zu einem prosperierenden Gemeinwesen gehören, strömten herbei, ergänzten einander und bildeten eine schöpferische, sich gegenseitig inspirierende Gemeinschaft. Diese Stadt ist Berlin bis heute geblieben. Sie steckt noch immer voller Möglichkeiten und ist für jeden, der das Herz dazu hat, eine Herausforderung.

Ich mag diese Stadt wie keine andere und so waren mir die Arbeiten zu diesem Bildband natürlich sehr willkommen. Mit sehenden Augen und natürlich meiner Kameraausrüstung streifte ich durch die Straßen und genoß Berlin in vollen Zügen. Ich hatte herrliche Begegnungen, entdeckte Altes und Neues, war mal begeistert, mal bedrückt und des öfteren amüsiert.

Mehr als einmal erging es mir wie damals, während meiner ersten Tage in Berlin. Ich fand mich in einem Straßenzug wieder, den ich nie zuvor betreten hatte, ich sprach mit Menschen, die ich nie zuvor gesehen hatte und hatte dennoch das Gefühl, keineswegs fremd zu sein. Es waren wundervolle Tage. Beim Blick durch den Sucher meiner Kamera erlebte ich in ungewöhnlicher Intensität die einmalige Atmosphäre dieser Stadt. Besonders freute mich, daß ich trotz neugieriger, ja bisweilen indiskreter Beobachtungen nur auf Wohlwollen und Verständnis stieß.

So konnten in diesem Bildband erfreulich viele Fotos Eingang finden, die auf das lebendige Berlin abzielen. Die Menschen vor der Kongreßhalle, die auf dem Wochenmarkt, die auf der Personenfähre, alle blieben sie herrlich unbefangen, alle nahmen sie – wohl Spektakuläreres gewohnt – von meiner Kamera kaum

Notiz. Die Berliner Gören drängten sich danach, abgelichtet zu werden und setzten dazu keineswegs sonntagsfromme Gesichter auf. Die aristokratisch, würdevoll blickende Dame im Vorgarten des Kurfürstendammcafés verzog trotz meines respektlosen Tuns keine Miene. Der Gammler zu Füßen der Kaiser-Wilhelm-Gedächtniskirche schlief weiter in den sonnigen Tag hinein und sogar der Seelefant im Zoologischen Garten tauchte besonders fotogen auf. Dank gebührt dem weißhaarigen Professor Hohenfels, der mir in der Philharmonie charmant, hilfsbereit und höchstpersönlich den besten Platz zum Fotografieren zuwies.

Bei den Bauwerken, der sogenannten toten Materie, bemühte ich mich durch den besonderen Blickwinkel, durch die ungewöhnliche Brennweite oder durch interessante Lichtverhältnisse um den gewissen Pfiff. Dabei möge mir das Reichstagsgebäude verzeihen, wenn ich die kantigen Formen durch meine Weitwinkeloptik abrundete und so die eigentlich schon immer umstrittene Architektonik gefälliger machte. Im Park des Charlottenburger Schlosses wartete ich Herbstnebel ab, um ein Foto voller Schwermut und Melancholie entstehen zu lassen. Ein wenig überrepräsentiert mögen in diesem Bildband die städtebaulichen Zeugnisse der Gründerjahre sein; aber was ist schon die sachlich kühle Front eines Hochhauses etwa im Märkischen Viertel gegen die schmuckbeladene, prunkvolle Fassade eines liebevoll restaurierten Wohnhauses aus der Zeit um die Jahrhundertwende?

Lieber Leser, ich hoffe, daß es mir gelungen ist, dem Gegenstand meiner Verehrung ein wenig auf den Leib zu rücken. Natürlich weiß ich, daß auch tausend Fotos nicht ausreichen würden, Berlin nur annähernd zu definieren. Aber gerade das ist es ja, was den besonderen Reiz ausmacht: Man wird diese faszinierende Stadt nie restlos erfassen können.

B.E.

My Berlin

The sigh arises from deep down inside the heart: It was back in 1964 when I moved to Berlin. In looking back at the years which have elapsed since then certain places and things stick out in my mind. I grow a bit sentimental. But after weighing all the pro's and con's I can still say to myself that moving to Berlin then was the right thing to do. I left all the others behind who were still undecided. Yes, you made the right move, I reassure myself. At the same time I must admit that I wasn't so enthused about the idea at the time. I came for more or less business reasons. It would be simple to cite motives which might appear more sophisticated and elevated. I could point out that there was an urgent demand for skilled workers in Berlin three years after the unfortunate errection of the Wall. I could discuss the city's status on a political front or focus on the political awareness particular to Berlin. Yes, I could go on and on mentioning one stereotyped cliché after another. But these years in Berlin have left their mark on me. I won't go into that now, however. It would leave a bitter aftertaste of pathos.

The initial attitude of scepticism toward my new domicile gradually dwindled. In the ensuing months sentiments of fondness for the place replaced the sobriety and detachment I'd felt earlier. Then, as though a spark had ignited, my feelings were kindled into flames of passion. I've long since realized that Berlin can't be mastered all at once. This takes time. And no one knows this better than those newcomers who later become the native patriots out of conviction.

The local Chamber of Commerce propagates Berlin's reputed lustrous façade. This does, in fact, exist. But the method of presentation in a superficial way is a problem for any other city too. This superficial image is by no means typical of Berlin. Berlin is no sumptuous beauty. Neither is it a city like Rome, Paris or Prague, lavishing in historical and monumental extravagance. Instead, Berlin is more like a woman: one wouldn't turn around to look at her, yet she exudes equally important virtues of warmth, motherliness and reliability.

In this respect, I had mixed feelings about Berlin in the beginning. I wasn't all that impressed by the so-called tourist attractions. All I'd heard about its being so metropolitan didn't turn out to be so dazzling after all. It was the people who lived here, though, the Berliners themselves, that convinced me, that raised Berlin to the status of a magnificent place. Berliners are, if I may make the compliment, open and tolerant in a way matched nowhere else in the world. A remark like, "Hey, what's he doing here?" made in reference to some stranger, is by no means an expression of distrust, rather of curiosity and interest – one is immediately accepted and integrated. Granted, there is no such thing as insincere formulas for politeness or a phoney sort of considerate behavior. This was illustrated once at the Winterfeldt Platz: A most determined women quipped to my face: "Pictures, you wanna take pictures here? If you had to live here, you wouldn't think this was such a nice place." The straightforwardness of the Berliners can be disarming. It is not seldom that it has left many an unaccustomed visitor from the provinces somewhat lost for words. The intent is never to hurt or do injury to someone. I highly value this sort of directness – a prerequisite for openness in any relationship.

Berlin is a relatively young city which has grown in tremendous proportions. In the past, the USA magically attracted many a restless soul to its shores. Similarly, Berlin was also a human melting pot of sorts. The USA earned the reputation of being the land of unlimited opportunity. Whoever wanted to become somebody in Germany had to come to Berlin. Innovators, intellectuals, artisans and artists – all the characters that constitute a prosperous community – such people seized the opportunity and came in droves to Berlin. Here they could compliment one another's talent and they formed an environment where mutual inspiration and creativity could flourish. Berlin has maintained this tradition even today. What it offers in opportunities is as great today as it was then. It presents a challenging milieu for the artistically inclined.

I feel about Berlin the way I feel about no other place. So it was sheer enjoyment working on this book. I strolled through the streets equipped with camera and wide open eyes and revelled in what I saw. I experienced wonderful encounters with people, discovered the old and the new. Sometimes I felt really excited about what I came across, other times somewhat dejected, but for the most part it was a fun experience.

It happened frequently that I felt the same as I did when I first came to Berlin. I'd be in a street lined with houses where I'd never been before. I'd talk with people I'd never seen before. Yet never once did I feel like a stranger. It was a beautiful experience. Looking through my camera lense I was able to comprehend in a short but intense time what an incredibly unique atmosphere Berlin has. It was a joy, a very positive experience to encounter people's well wishes and under-standing throughout the entire venture – despite several instances where I was a bit too curious or even indiscrete.

And so many photos found their way into this picture book whose purpose it is to present a living countenance of Berlin. The people in front of the Congress Hall, at the market place, on the ferry boat – all acted quite naturally and hardly noticed my camera. – They were probably used to more spectacular things. The kids pushed and shoved to get there picture taken and left expressions of facial piety out of the poses. The aristocratic dignified lady sitting out front in a café on the Kurfürstendamm didn't bat an eyelash – despite my somewhat discourteous fumbling around. The bums that hang out around the steps of the Kaiser Wilhelm Memorial Church went on sleeping undisturbed on that sunny day. And even the sea elephant in the zoo turned out to be most photogenic. Thanks is due to the white haired Professor Hohenfels, a gracious, helpful man who personally disclosed the best spot in the Philharmonic to take pictures from.

I tried to lend some nuance to the photos of buildings, the so-called inanimate matter, by employing a different angle, an unusual focal length or some interesting lighting technique. In this respect, I hope the Reichstag building will forgive me for rounding off its edges with my wide angle lense. In doing so I've rendered a more pleasant version of this piece of architecture which has always been a subject of controversy. I waited for the autumnal fog to set in in order to photograph the park of the Charlottenburg Palace in a melancholy mood. It may seem that this book devotes too much attention to edifaces dating from the "Gründerjahre" (Founding Years). But how could one equate the splendidly decorated façade of a lovingly refurbished appartment house from the turn of the century with an objective, technical front side of some high rise in the modern Märkisches Viertel section of the city?

Dear Reader, I hope I've been able to acquaint you more closely with this object of my adoration. Of course, I realize that thousands of pictures wouldn't even begin to define this phenomenon, Berlin. But that is exactly what's so captivating about the place – one will never be able to completely comprehend what this fascinating city is all about.

B.E.

Berlins U-Bahn verkehrt auf Teilstrecken auch über der Erde,
so wie hier vor dem Postscheckamt.

Some subway stretches run above ground – as do these tracks
in front of the postal check building.

Architektonische Glanzlichter
aus vergangenen Zeiten:
Links der Kuppelturm
des Charlottenburger Schlosse
rechts das Teehaus Belvedere

Architectural highlights
from days past:
Left, the dome shaped tower
of the Charlottenburg Palace,
ight, the Belvedere Tea House.

Als repräsentativstes Bauwerk preußischer Vergangenheit auf Berliner Boden gilt heute das Schloß Charlottenburg.

The Charlottenburg Palace is today the most typical building representing
the Prussian past which stands on Berlin soil.

Gegenlicht verzaubert:
Das mächtige Reiterstand-
bild des Großen Kurfürsten
im Schloßhof Charlottenburg.

The magical effect of
shooting against the light:
The great equestrian statue
of the Great Elector in the
courtyard of the Charlottenburg Palace.

Herbstnebel im Schloßpark Charlottenburg.
Autumn fog in the park of the Charlottenburg Palace.

Am Rande der Stadt sind mehrere neue Wohnviertel entstanden:
Links eine Aufnahme aus der Gropiusstadt, rechts zwei Fotos aus dem Märkischen Viertel.

Numerous housing projects have sprung up on the edge of the city:
On the left, a shot of the Gropiusstadt; on the right, two pictures from the Märkisches Viertel.

Die alte Pumpe und das prunkvolle Fensteroval bilden einen
wohltuenden Kontrast zur modernen Sachlichkeit.

The old water pump and the splendid oval window provide a
pleasant contrast to modern realism.

Eine wahrhaft noble Dame –
und ein gelungener Schnappschuß.

A truly noble lady –
and a snapshot which didn't turn out bad at all.

Dolce far niente
auf berlinisch.

The Berlin version of il dolce
far niente, taking life easy.

Links eine Aussichtsplattform an der Mauer,
rechts ein Teilabschnitt der Sektorengrenze zwischen den Bezirken
Berlin-Mitte und Kreuzberg.

Left, a lookout platform at the Wall,
right, a section of the boarder between the districts
of Berlin-Mitte and Kreuzberg.

Pompös und prunkbeladen wie ehedem
wurde das Reichstagsgebäude wiedererrichtet.

The Reichstag building was restored
in its former pompous, ostentatious style.

Bittere Berliner Realitäten:
Links eine unpassierbare Brücke, die Glienicker Brücke,
rechts ein unpassierbares Tor, das Brandenburger Tor.

The bitter facts in Berlin:
On the left, an impassable bridge, the Glienicker Bridge;
on the right, an impassable gate, the Brandenburg Gate.

Was ist es, was die Berliner Flohmärkte so liebenswert macht?
Ist es das amüsierte Publikum,
der so herrlich unnütze Kitsch,
der verstaubte Trödel oder die Pfiffigkeit der Händler?

What is it about the fleamarkets in Berlin that makes them so charming?
The customers having a good time?
The totally useless junk items?
The second hand wares all covered with dust?
Or the way the shrewd vendors pedal their bargains?

Die Königskolonaden bilden eine repräsentative Pforte zum Schöneberger Kleistpark.

The king's colonnade constitute a typical gatew leading into the Kleistpark in Schöneberg.

Das unmittelbar an der Spree gelegene Schloß Bellevue ist ein Juwel
unter den Berliner Schlössern.

Bellevue Palace, located directly on the banks of the Spree, is a jewel
among Berlin's palaces.

Stätten der Musen:
Links oben das gläserne Viereck der Neuen Nationalgalerie,
links unten die Akademie der Künste
und rechts die Front des Theaters des Westens.

HANC DOMVM ARTIS COLENDAE CAVSA CONDIDIT.
ANNO MDCCCLXXXXVI BERNHARD SEHRING.

Abodes of the Muses:
Above left: the glass quadrangle of the New National Gallery,
below left: the Academy of Art
and right: in front of the Theater des Westens.

In der Philharmonie

Inside of the Philharmonic

Die Berliner Museen sind weltberühmt:
Links oben im Schloß Charlottenburg, links unten in der Neuen Nationalgalerie,
rechts im Dahlemer Museum.

The museums of Berlin are famous all over the world:
Above left, in the Charlottenburg Palace, below left, in the New National Gallery,
right, in the Museum at Dahlem.

Zu den größten Kostbarkeiten der Berliner Museen
zählt die über 3000 Jahre alte Kalksteinbüste der Nofretete.

The limestone bust of Nefertiti, over 3,000 years old,
is classified among the very valuable items housed in Berlin's museums.

George Grosz schuf 1926 das Gemälde „Stützen der Gesellschaft", das jetzt in der Neuen Nationalgalerie hängt.

In 1926 George Grosz executed the painting "Pillars of Society", which is now in the New National Gallery.

Ein Hauch von Exklusivität umweht den alljährlich stattfindenden
Moderenntag auf der Trabrennbahn in Mariendorf.

An exclusive scent whiffs across the harness racetrack in Mariendorf
which hosts an annual fashion racing day.

Das neue ICC Berlin ist eines der größten Kongreßzentren Europas.
The new ICC Berlin is one of the largest convention halls in Europe.

Eines der Berli-
ner Wahrzeichen
ist der Funkturm.

The Radio Tower
is one of Berlin's
landmarks.

Haveleis

Ice on the
Havel River

Einsamkeit, Stille und ein
wenig Befangenheit strahlen
die beiden Fotos auf dieser
Doppelseite aus:
Links eine Aufnahme vom
Friedhof Wilmersdorf,
rechts das Bild eines alten
Landhauses in Lübars.

The photos on these two pages elicit lonliness, peace and quiet and shyness: Left – a shot of the Wilmersdorf Cemetery, right – a picture of an old country home in Lübars.

Ihre Ausflugslokale lieben die Berliner
ganz besonders.

Berliners are especially fond of their café-restaurants
when they go on outings.

Berliner Junge[n]
die sind richtig

The boys in
Berlin, they're a[ll]
right ...

Großstadtidylle:
Mundharmonikaspieler in der Karl-Marx-Straße.

Idyllic scene in the city:
A harmonica player on the Karl-Marx-Straße.

Berlin ist die größte Industriestadt
zwischen Paris und Moskau.

Berlin is the largest industrial city
between Paris and Moscow.

Impressionen aus Wilmersdorf: Links die russisch-orthodoxe Kathedrale,
rechts ein Abschnitt der Stadtautobahn mit den drei Schornsteinen
des Fernheizkraftwerkes an der Mecklenburgischen Straße.

Impressions from Wilmersdorf: Left, the Russian Orthodox Cathedral,
right, a section of the inner city turnpike showing the three chimneys
of the district heating plant on the Mecklenburgische Straße.

Im Herzen der Stadt befindet sich der Zoologische Garten mit seinem beliebten Kaffeegarten und seinem Musikpavillon.

The Zoo lies in downtown Berlin. On its grounds are a popular outdoor café and a pavillon where concerts are held.

A picture full of poetry:
Tuaillon's bronze Amazon in the wintry Tiergarten.

Die Pfaueninsel ist ein beliebtes Ausflugsziel ...
The Pfaueninsel (Peacock Island) is a favorite outing spot ...

... und nur mit der Fähre erreichbar.
... and is accessable only by ferry.

Sonnenuntergang an der Havel
Sunset on the Havel

Die alte Dorf-
kirche in Britz.

The old village
church in Britz.

Die Kinder sind unsere Hoffnung ...
The children are our hope ...

... aber auch die Alten dürfen wir nicht vergessen.
... and yet not forget our responsibility to the elderly.

Zwei Bilder, die märkische Schwermut erahnen lassen:
Links das Jagdschloß Grunewald,
rechts die Havel.

Two pictures which evoke a sense of melancholy in the Mark:
Left, the Grunewald Hunting Castle,
right, the Havel.

Fremdländisches in Berlin:
Links die pakistanische Moschee in Wilmersdorf,
rechts türkische Gastarbeiter in Kreuzberg.

A touch of the foreign in Berlin:
The Pakistan Mosque in Wilmersdorf on the left,
Turkish laborers in Kreuzberg on the right.

Monumentale Zeugnisse der jüngeren Vergangenheit:
Links die Siegessäule,
rechts das Bismarckdenkmal.

Monumental witnesses to the recent past:
The Victory Column on the left,
the Bismarck Memorial on the right.

Berlins vornehmster Flanier-
boulevard, die Straße Unter den
Linden, befindet sich jetzt in der
östlichen Stadthälfte.
Im Vordergrund das ehemalige
Zeughaus und jetzige Museum für
Deutsche Geschichte, im Hinter-
grund der alles überragende
Fernsehturm am Alexanderplatz.

The most distinguished place to
go for a stroll in Berlin, the street
called "Unter den Linden", now lies
in the eastern part of the city.
In the foreground the Museum of
German History, formerly the
armory; in the background the
TV-Tower at the Alexander Platz
towering above everything which
lies below.

Am Fuße des Fernsehturms:
Berliner Gören.

At the base of the TV-Tower:
Berlin children.

Berlin, Straße Unter den Linden:
Die ehemalige Neue Wache ist heute Mahnmal für die Opfer des Faschismus und Militarismus (links),
die Sowjetische Botschaft (rechts) befindet sich nahe dem Brandenburger Tor.

Berlin, Unter den Linden:
What was once the New Guard House serves today as a memorial for the victims of Fascism and militarism
(left), the Soviet Embassy is located in the vicinity of the Brandenburg Gate (right).

Charlottenburg bietet noch viel Hinterhofromantik ...
Charlottenburg still offers lots of backyard romanticism ...

... und eine ganze Menge Gemütlichkeit.
... and lots of inviting places to sit and relax.

Nostalgie par excellence:
Die beiden Fotos dieser Doppelseite wurden erst in diesen Tagen aufgenommen.
Ebensogut hätten sie freilich bereits Ende des vorigen Jahrhunderts entstehen können.

Sentimental yearning for the past par excellence:
Both pictures on these two pages were taken recently.
They could just as well date from the close of the 19th Century.

Viel Liebe und Sorgfalt wurde aufgewandt, um diese herrliche Fassade
in der Klopstockstraße wieder im alten Glanze leuchten zu lassen.

A lot of love and care went into the restoration of the magnificent façade
of this dwelling in the Klopstockstraße to its former luster.

Liebenswertes aus alter Zeit:
Links einer der Kandelaber vor dem Berlin-Museum,
rechts das prachtvolle Portal zu Riehmers Hofgarten.

Pleasant remnants of days gone by:
On the left, one of the lanterns in front of the Berlin-Museum,
on the right, the splendid portal of Riehmer's Hofgarten.

Der Kurfürstendamm – das ist ein Name, der die Herzen höher schlagen läßt.
Wie der Blick vom „i-Punkt" des Europa-Centers zeigt,
verläuft Berlins Prachtboulevard keineswegs schnurgerade (Abb. rechts).
Den Höhepunkt an pulsierendem Leben erreicht er an der Stelle,
wo er die Joachimstaler Straße kreuzt (Abb. links).

The Kurfürstendamm – that's a name that makes the heart beat stronger.
As one can see from the "i-Punkt" on top of the Europa-Center,
Berlin's pace-setter boulevard of splendor by no means runs as straight as an arrow (right).
The Kurfürstendamm attains its peak of activity
where it intersects with the Joachimstaler Straße (left).

Großstadtverkehr:
Warten an der Bushaltestelle ...
Warten auf ein Taxi am Flughafen Tegel ...

Traffic in the city:
Waiting at the bus stop ...
Waiting for a taxi at Tegel Airport ...

... und endlich unterwegs
im Doppeldeckerbus.

... and finally things get rolling
in the double decker bus.

Berlin ist eine Stadt der Messen, Kongresse und Ausstellungen:
Links die Kongresshalle, die 1957 anläßlich der „Internationalen Bauausstellung" errichtet wurde,
rechts der Funkturm, zu dessen Füßen sich das Messegelände mit dem neuen ICC erstreckt.

Berlin is a city where many trade fairs, conventions and exhibitions are held:
Left, the Kongresshalle (Congress hall), errected in 1957 as part of the "International Building Exhibition";
right the Radio Tower. At its base the trade fair grounds extend over to the new ICC complex.

Kontraste:
Im Vordergrund die russisch-orthodoxe Kathedrale in Wilmersdorf,
im Hintergrund das neue Hochhaus der BFA.

Contrasts:
The Russian Orthodox Cathedral in Wilmersdorf in the foreground;
in the background the new, many storeyed BFA building.

rlinischer geht
nicht mehr!

hard to find
ything more
ical of Berlin
n this!

Das berühmte
Caféhaus
Möhring an der
Ecke Kurfürsten-
damm/Uhland-
straße.

The well-known
Café Möhring at
the corner of the
Kurfürstendamm
and Uhland-
straße.

Der Autor

Bernd Ehrig wurde 1944 in Hanau/Main geboren. Um seine beruflichen Kenntnisse als Druckfachmann zu vertiefen, siedelte er 1964 nach Berlin um, volontierte dort in einem der größten Druckereibetriebe und betätigte sich anschließend in leitender Funktion in einem Offsetbetrieb. Außerhalb seiner beruflichen Tätigkeit verschrieb er sich mit Leib und Seele der Fotografie. 1970, gerade sechsundzwanzigjährig, trat er mit seinem ersten großen Bildband zum Thema „Berlin" an die Öffentlichkeit. Der Erfolg dieser Publikation war sogleich beachtlich. Ermutigt schickte sich Bernd Ehrig an, diesem ersten Fotoband alsbald weitere folgen zu lassen.

Im Jahre 1977 schließlich verband Bernd Ehrig seine beruflichen Kenntnisse mit seinen persönlichen Neigungen und wurde selbständiger Verleger. Seiner großen Leidenschaft aber, der Fotografie, blieb er treu, so daß nichts naheliegender war, als im eigenen Verlag den hier vorliegenden Bildband erscheinen zu lassen.

The author

Bernd Ehrig was born in 1944 in Hanau on the Main. He moved to Berlin in 1964 to further his competence as a printing specialist and worked on a non-salaried basis for one of the largest printing concerns in Berlin. Following that he held a supervisory position in an offset printing company. Beyond his work in the printing business he devoted himself with body and soul to photography. In 1970, having just turned 26, he published his first picture book on Berlin. This book turned out to be an instant success. Encouraged by this, Bernd Ehrig began preparation on further picture books.

Finally, in 1977, Bernd Ehrig combined professional competence with personal propensity and began to do his own publishing. He has remained faithful to his passionate interest, photography, so that nothing was more important to him than to have this picture book published by his own company.